Mania Art by
Jennene C. Obremski

Jennene C. Obremski Copyright © 2016 Jennene
Obremski All rights reserved.
ISBN: **10: 1535589620**
 ISBN- **13: 978-1535589628**

Table of Contents

Mania Art by Jennene C. Obremski

Table of Contents

Table of Contents

Mania Art by Jennene C. Obremski

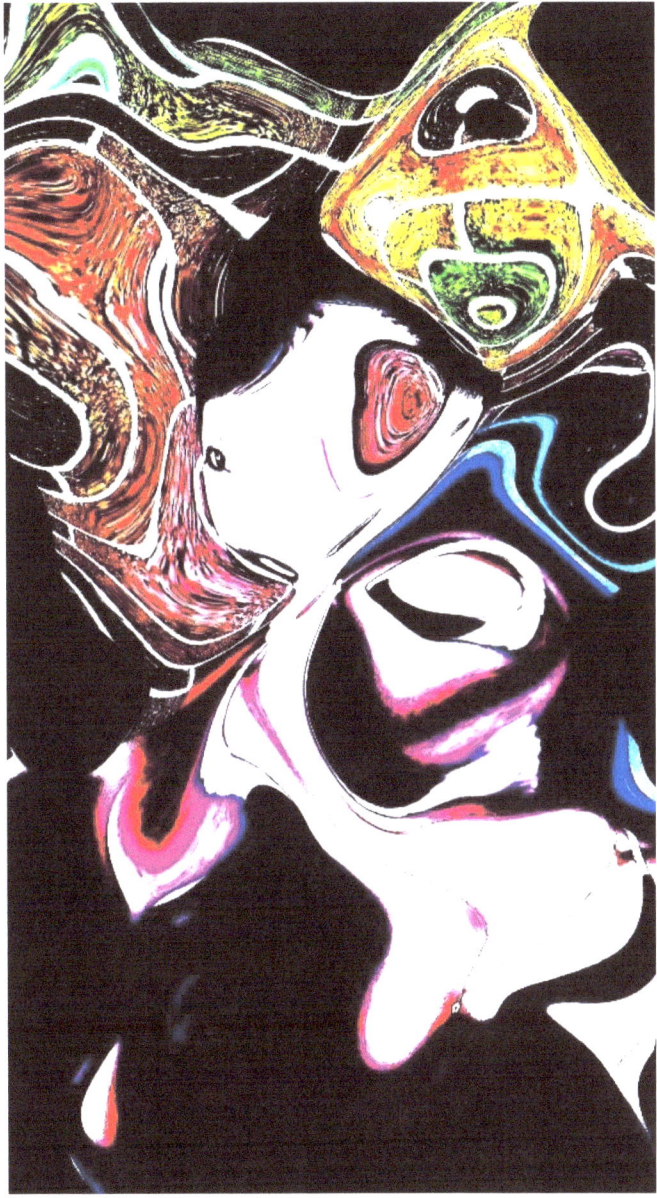

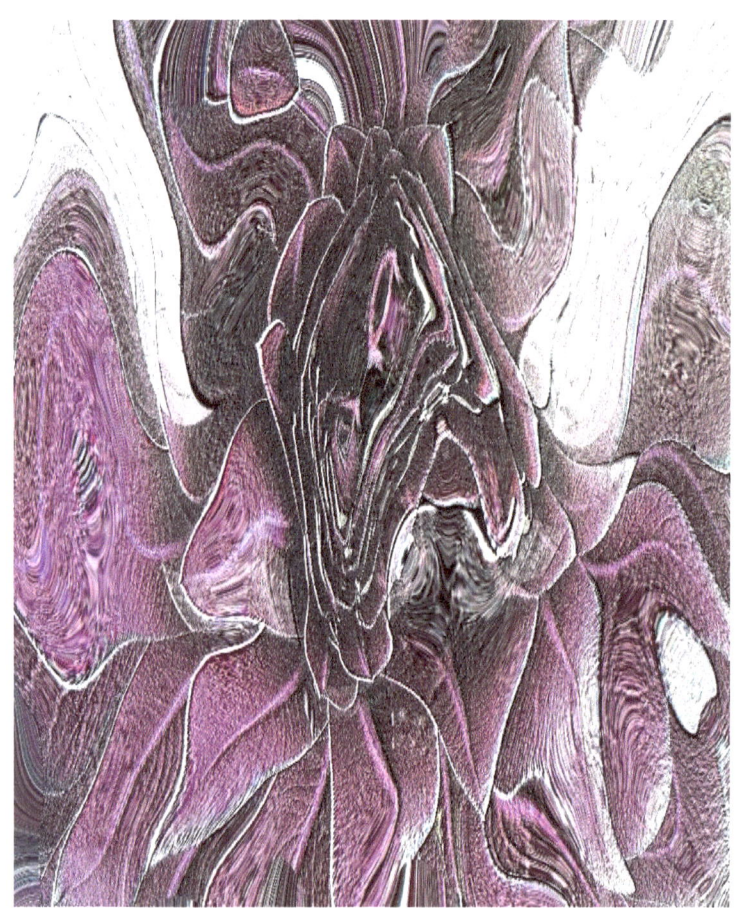

Mania Art by Jennene C. Obremski

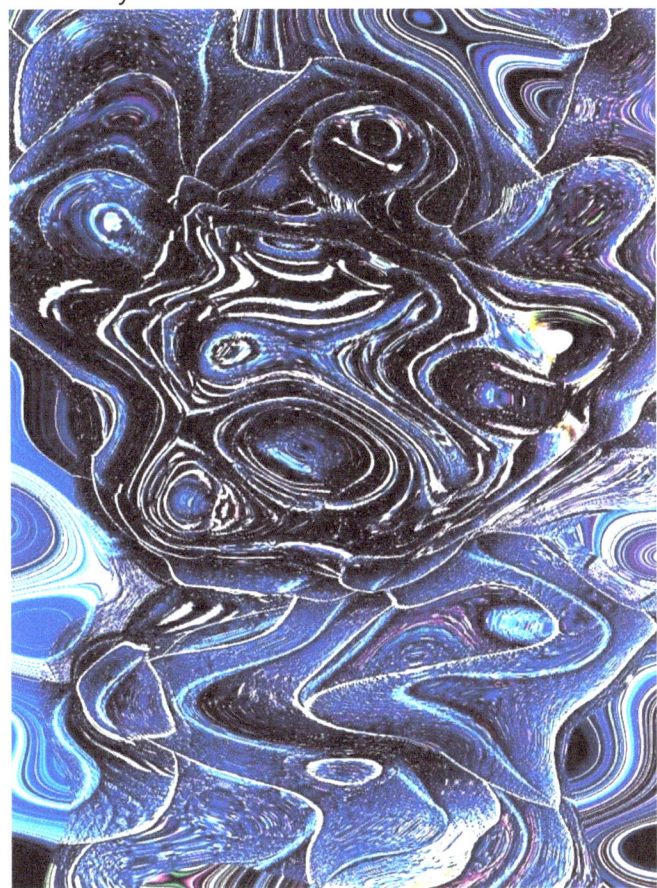

JENNENE OBREMSKI

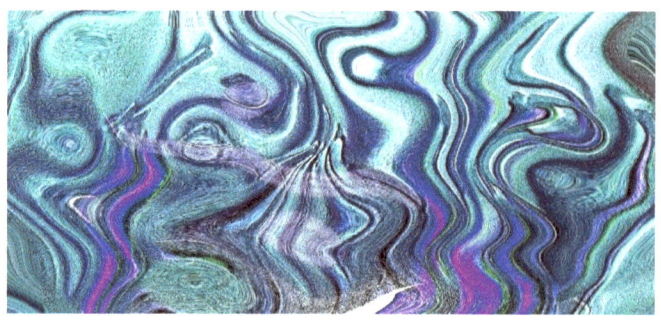

Mania Art by Jennene C. Obremski

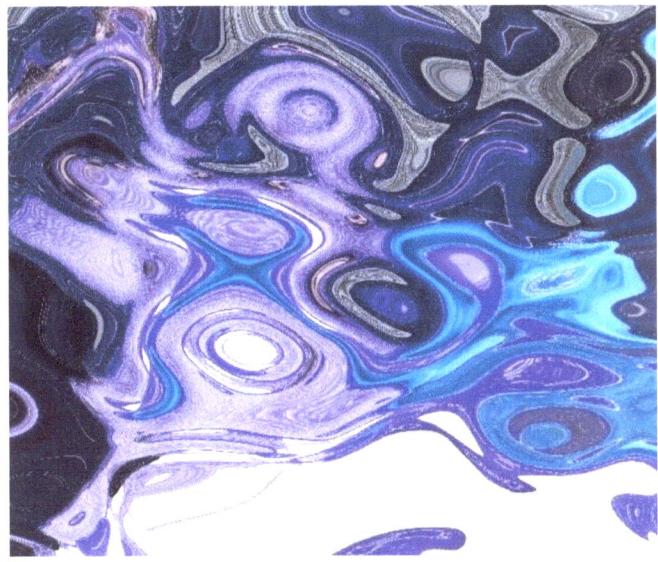

JENNENE OBREMSKI

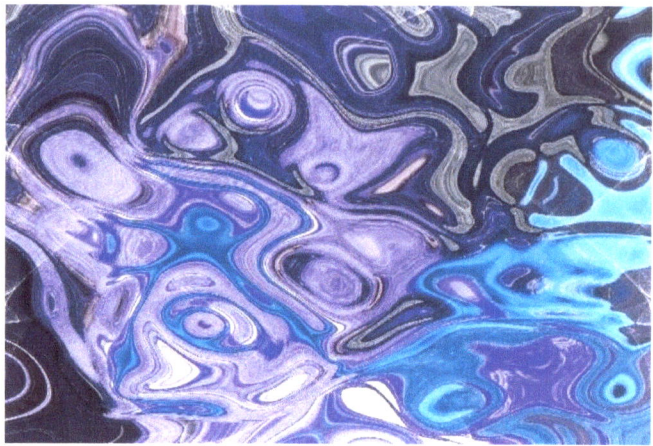

Mania Art by Jennene C. Obremski

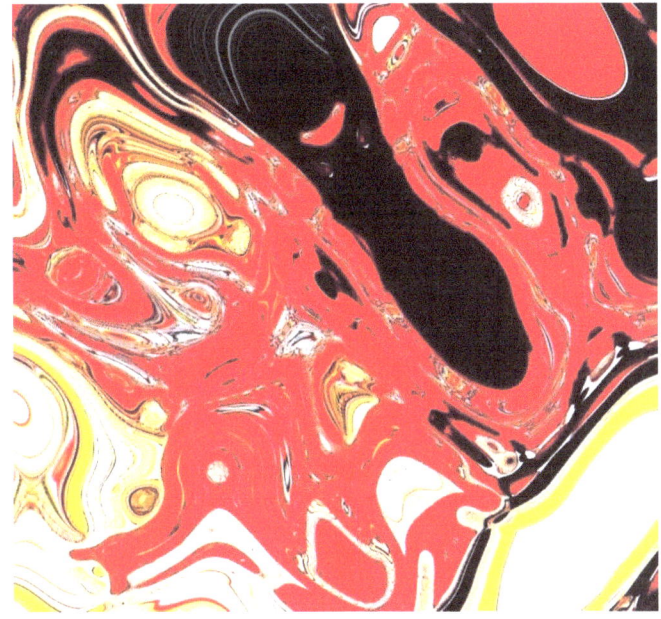

JENNENE OBREMSKI

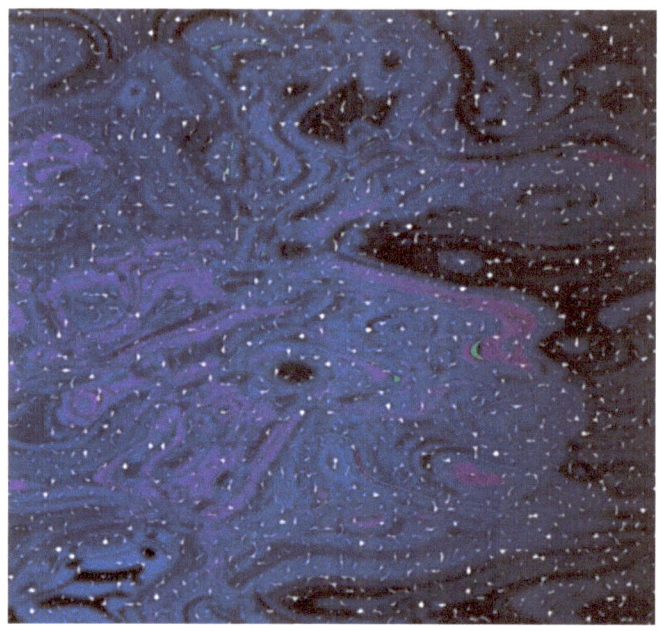

Mania Art by Jennene C. Obremski

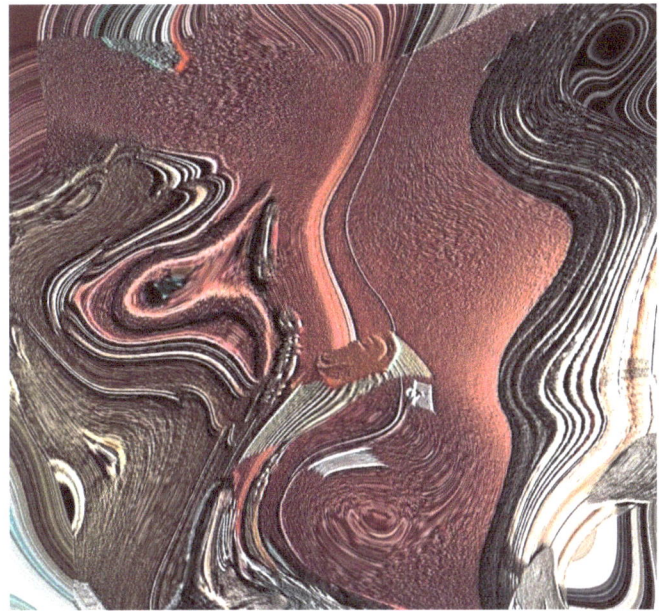

JENNENE OBREMSKI

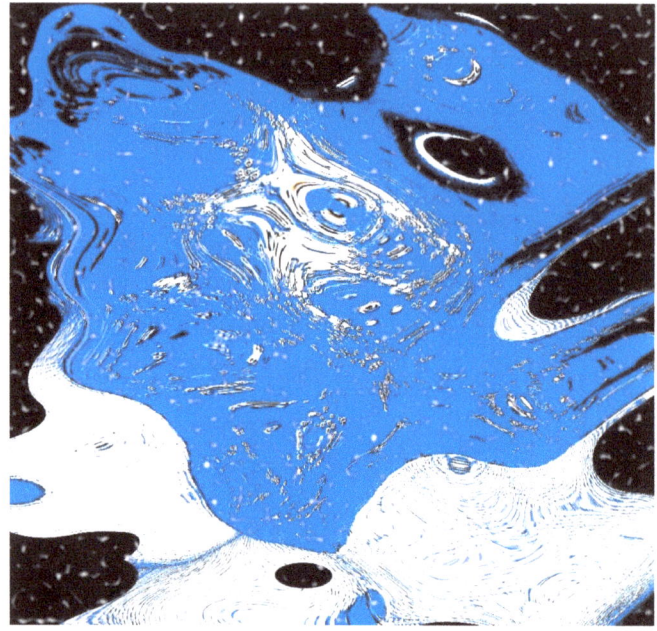

Mania Art by Jennene C. Obremski

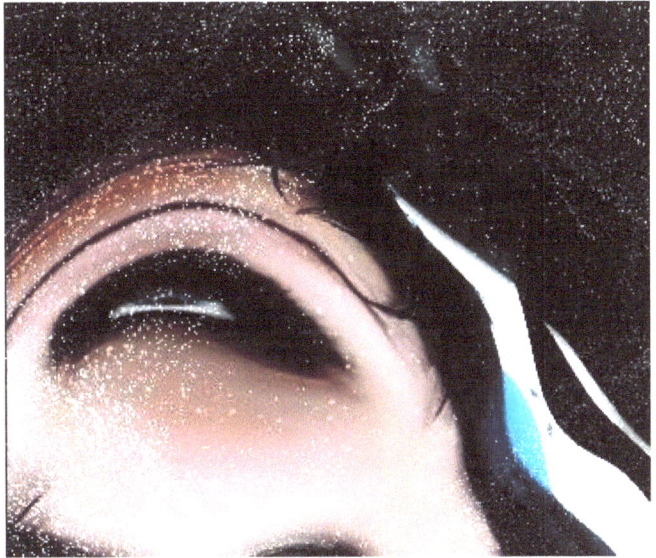

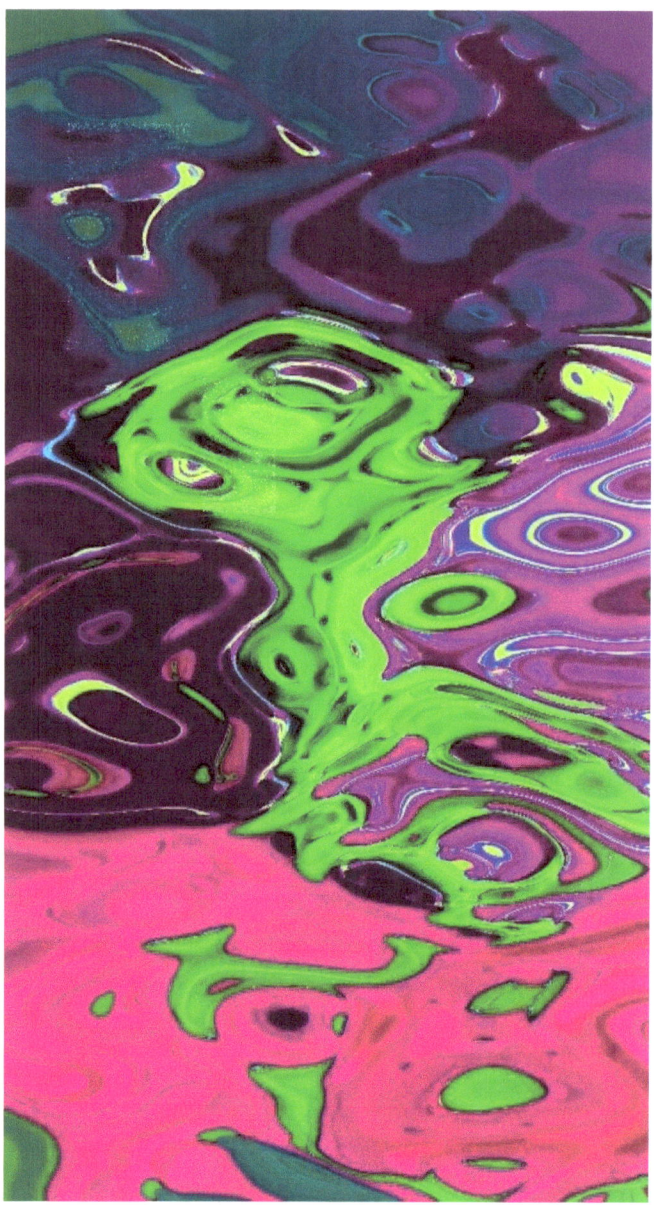

Mania Art by Jennene C. Obremski

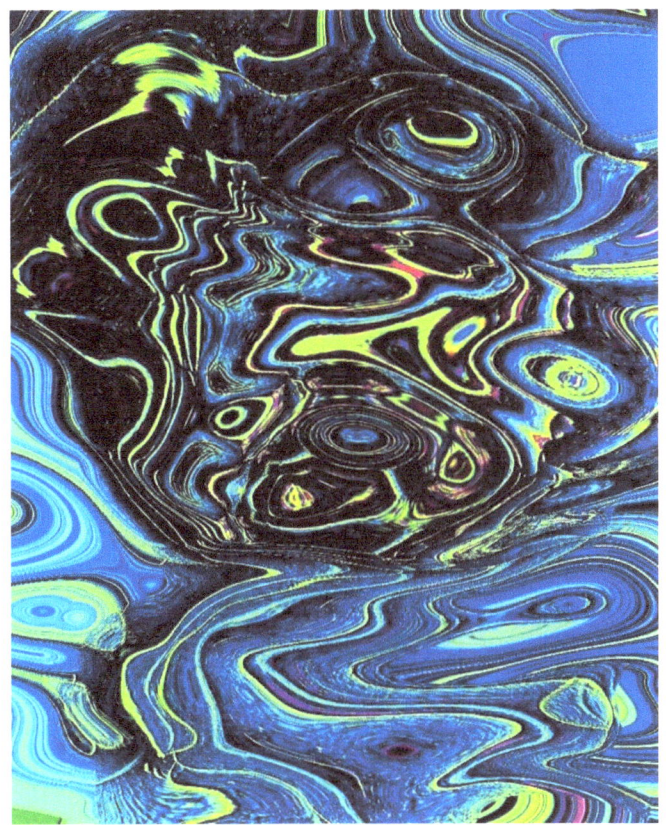

JENNENE OBREMSKI

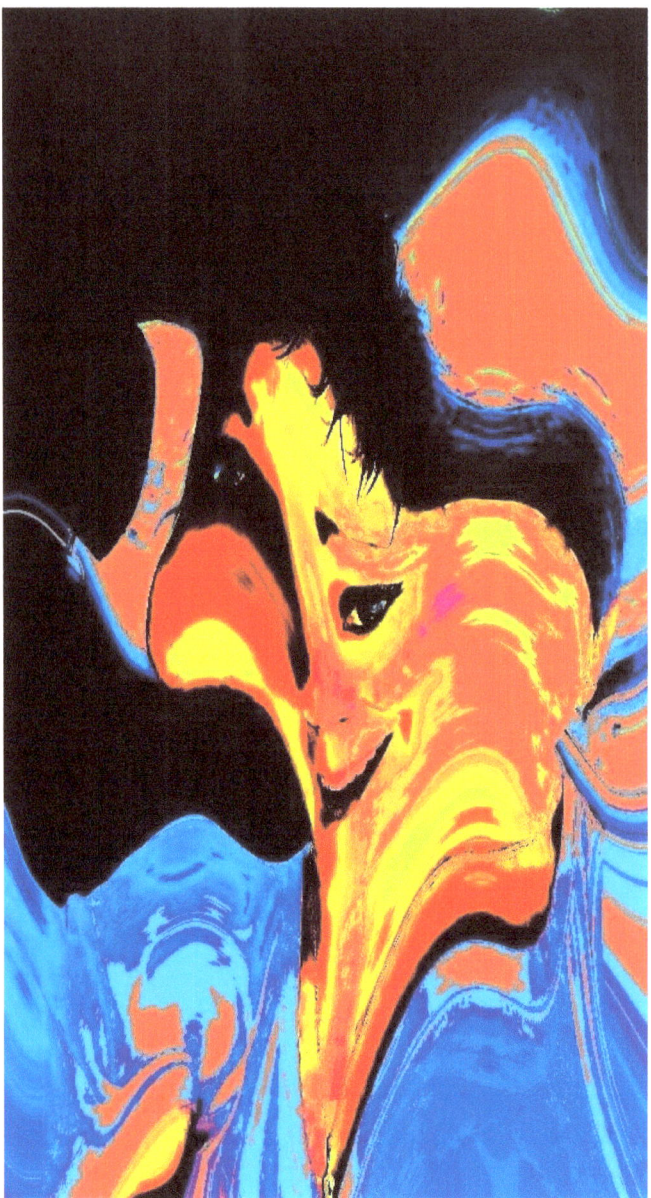

Mania Art by Jennene C. Obremski

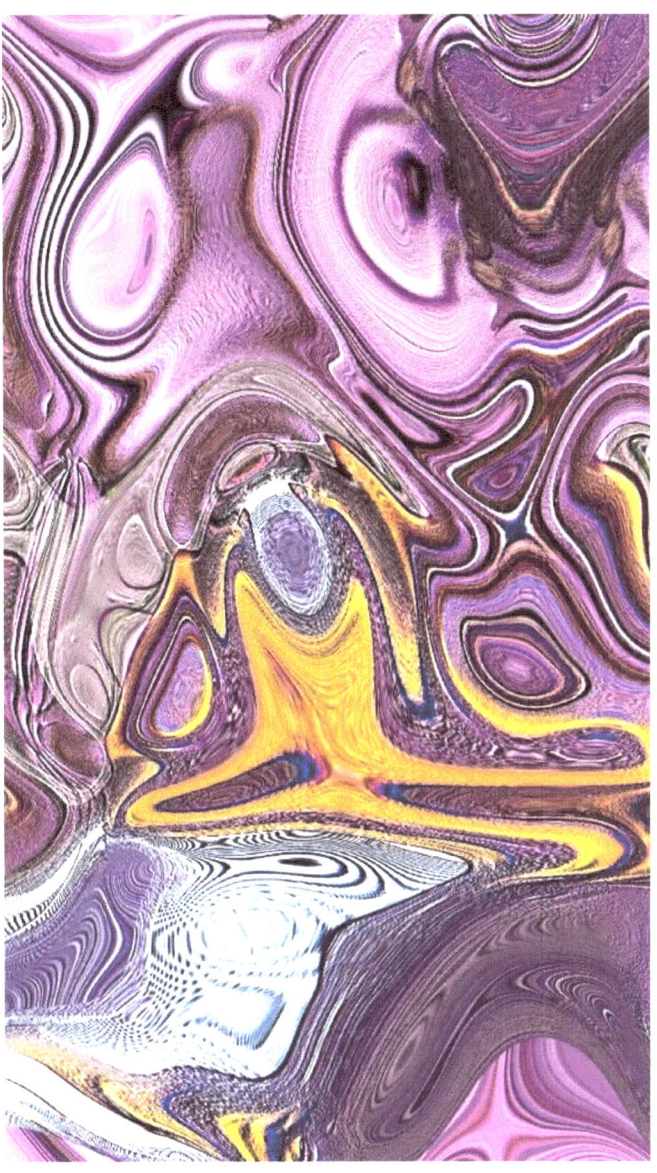

JENNENE OBREMSKI

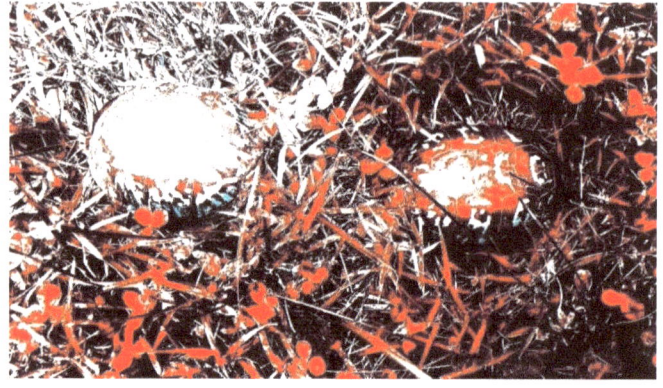

Mania Art by Jennene C. Obremski

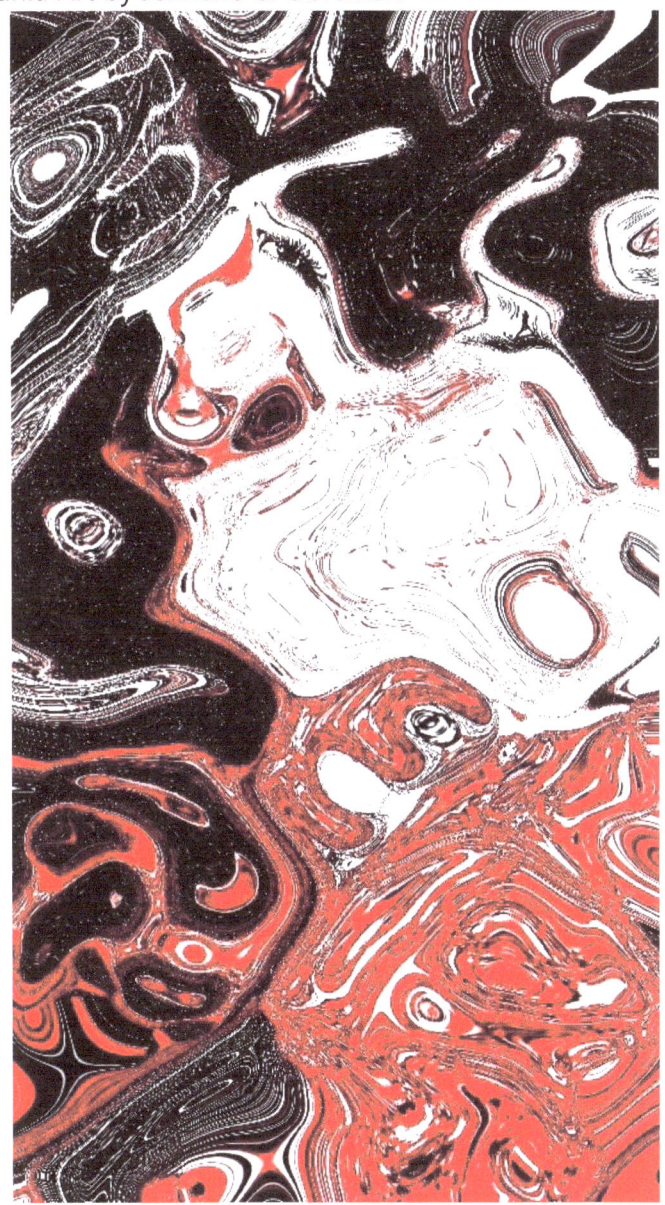

JENNENE OBREMSKI

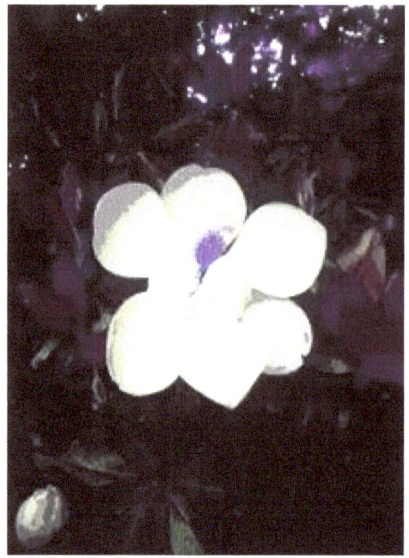

Mania Art by Jennene C. Obremski

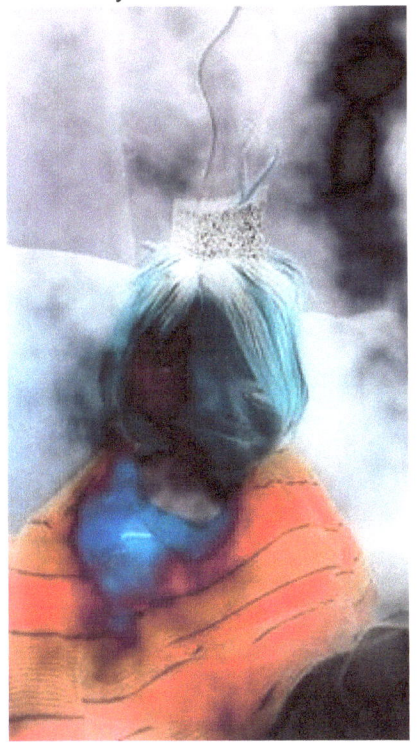

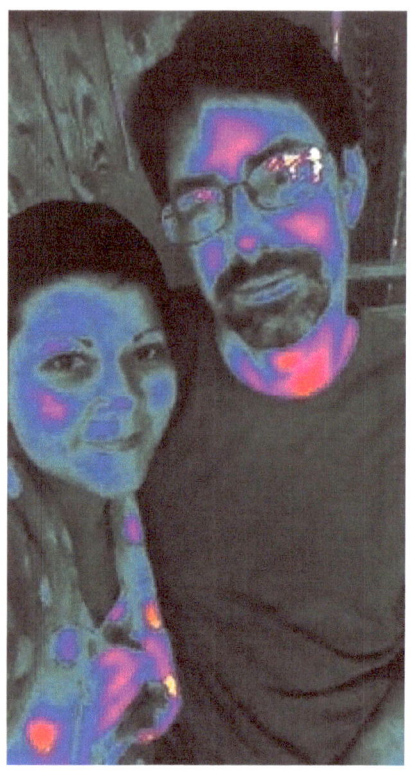

Mania Art by Jennene C. Obremski

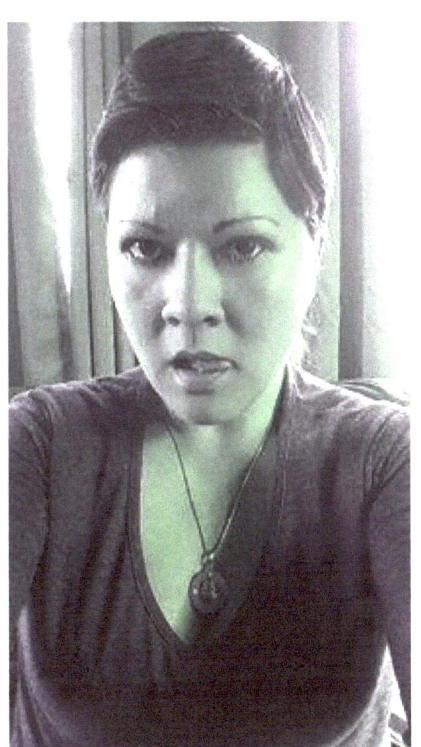

JENNENE OBREMSKI

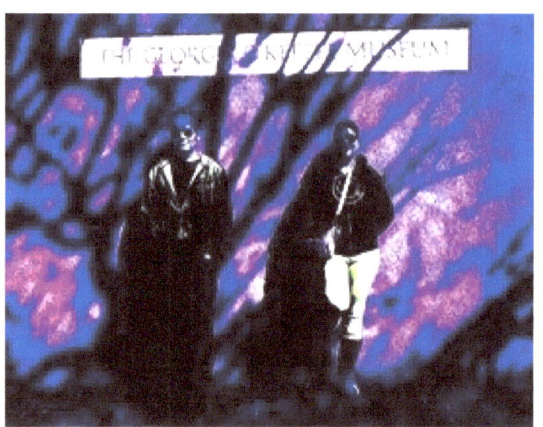

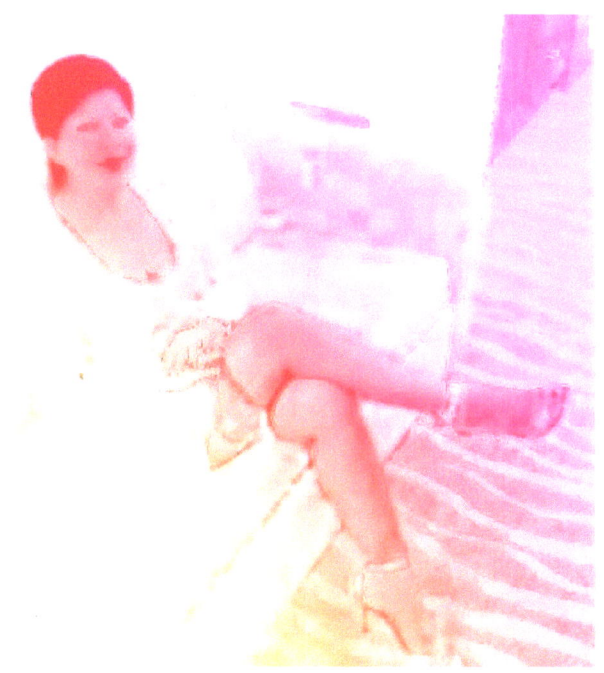

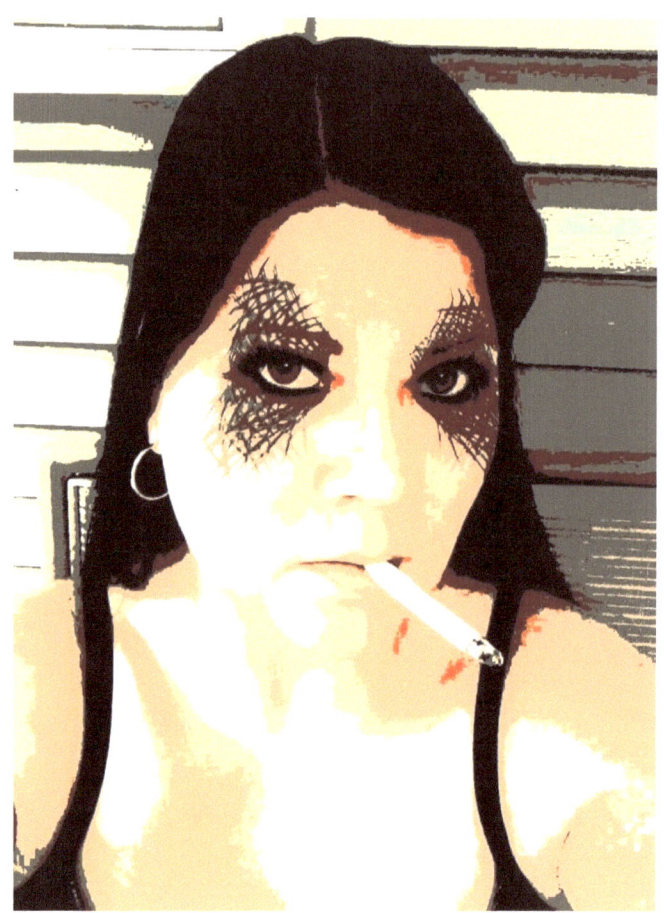

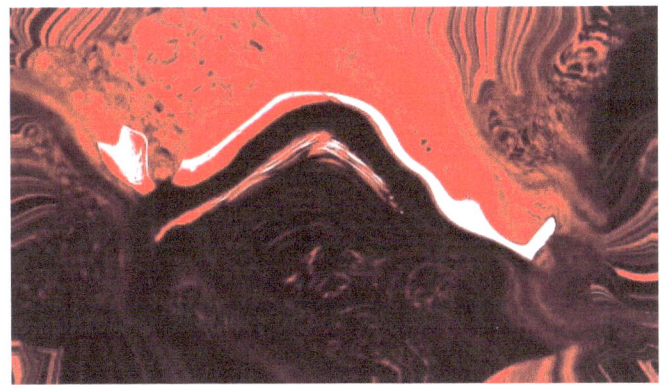

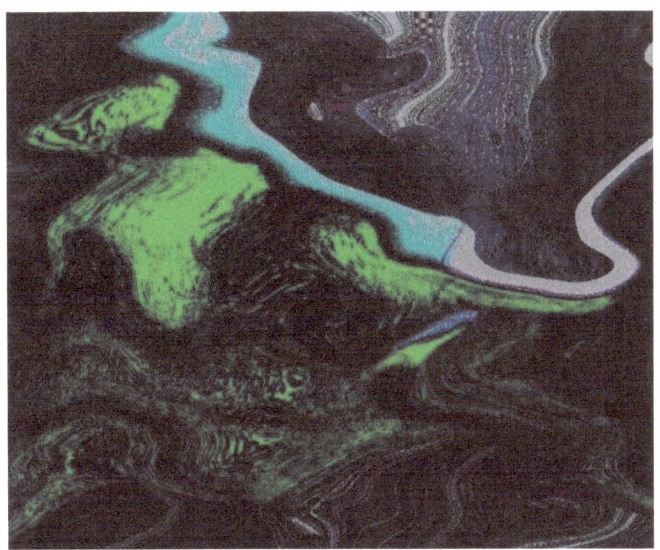

29

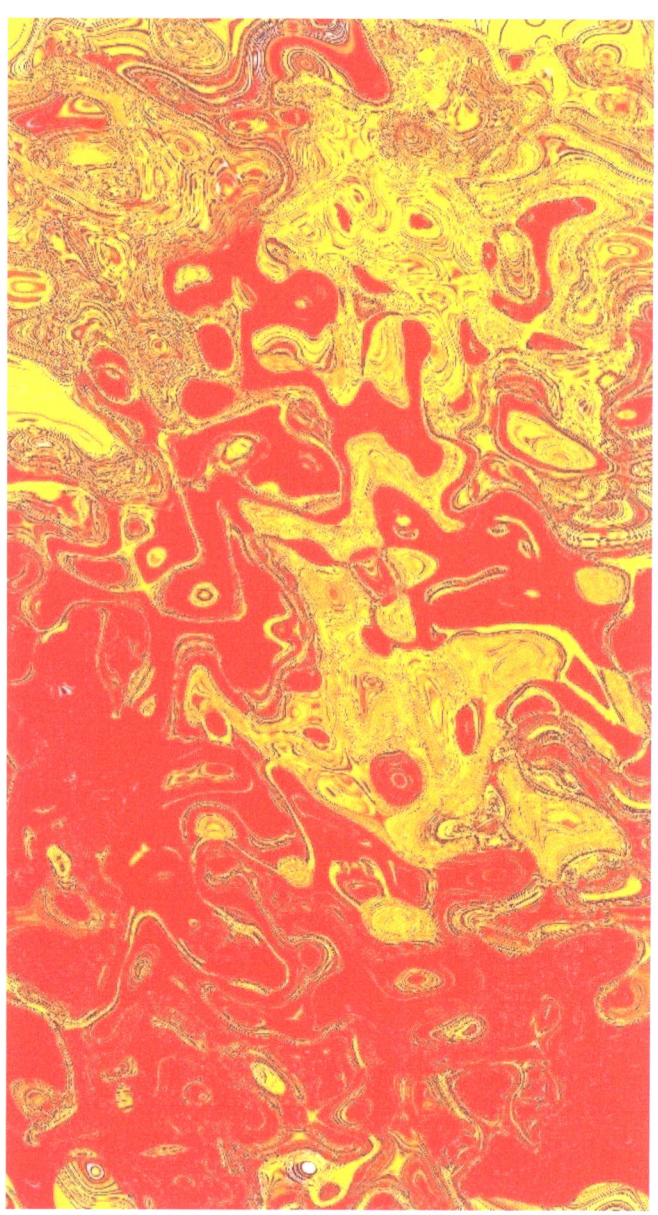

Mania Art by Jennene C. Obremski

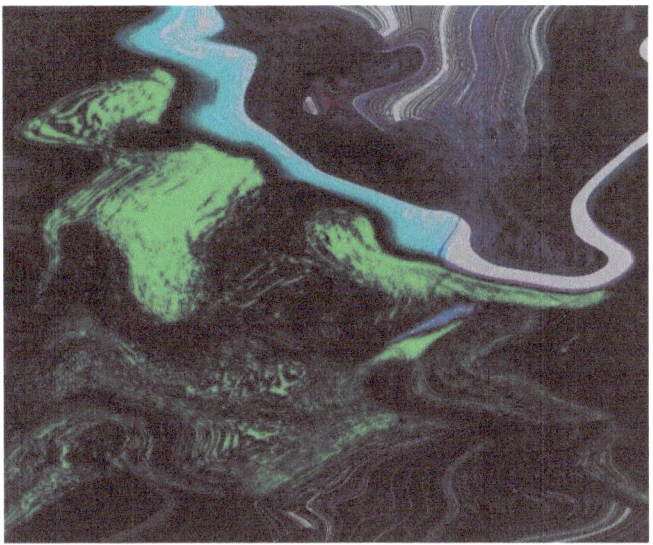

JENNENE OBREMSKI

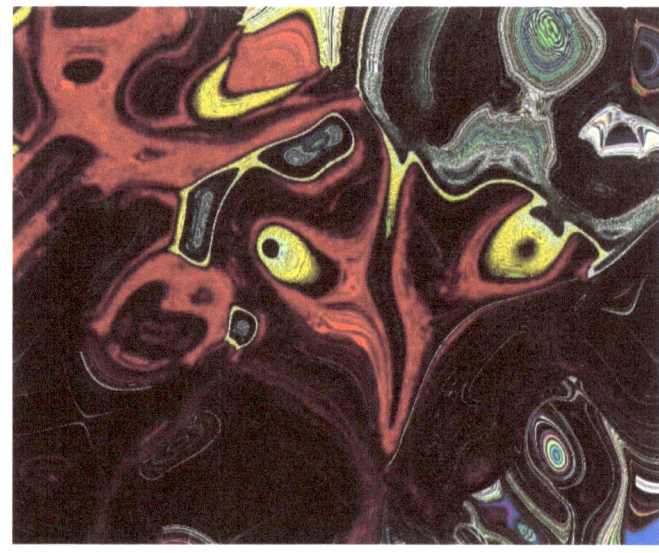

Mania Art by Jennene C. Obremski

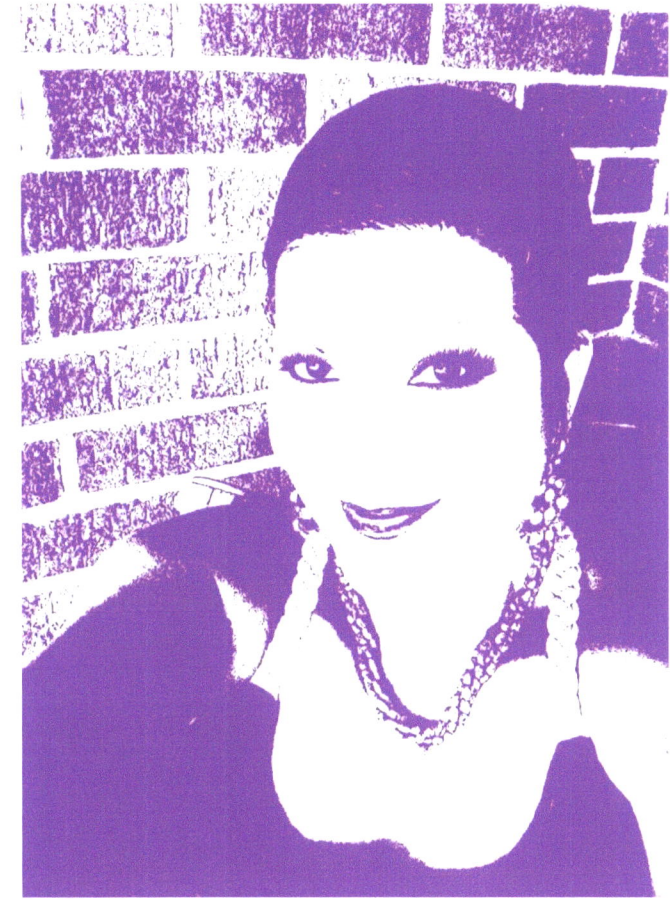

JENNENE OBREMSKI

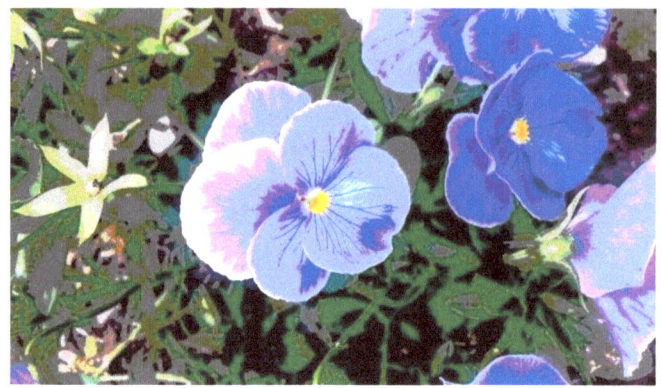

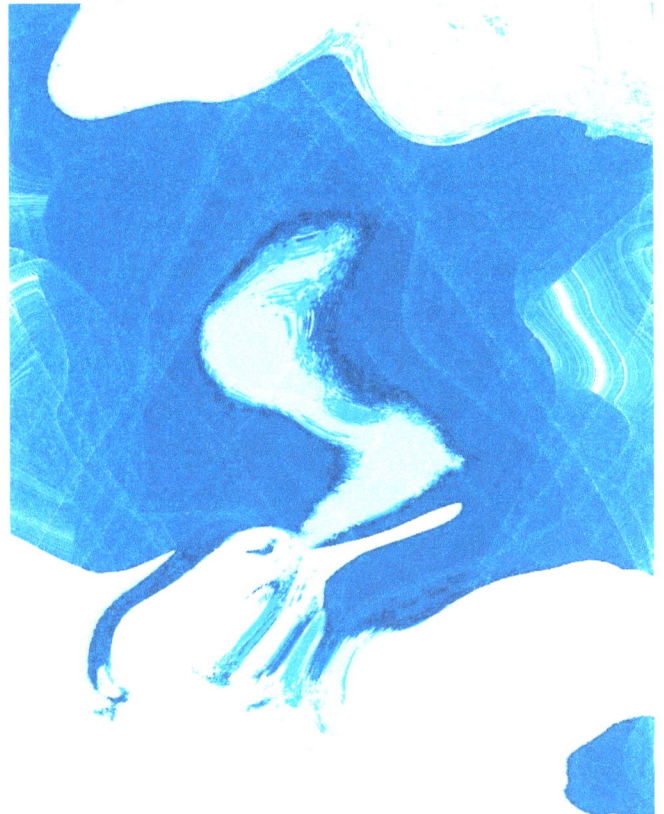

JENNENE OBREMSKI

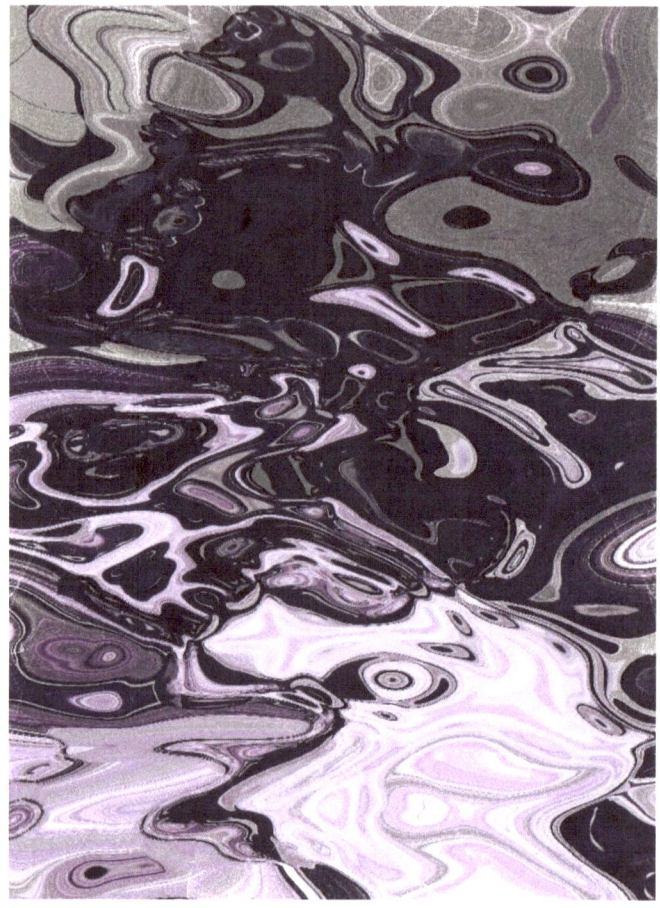

Mania Art by Jennene C. Obremski

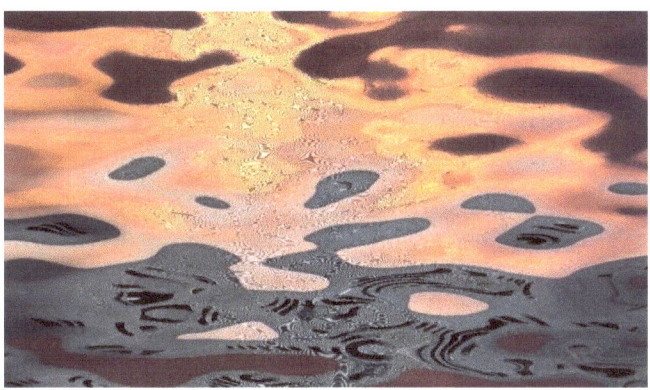

JENNENE OBREMSKI

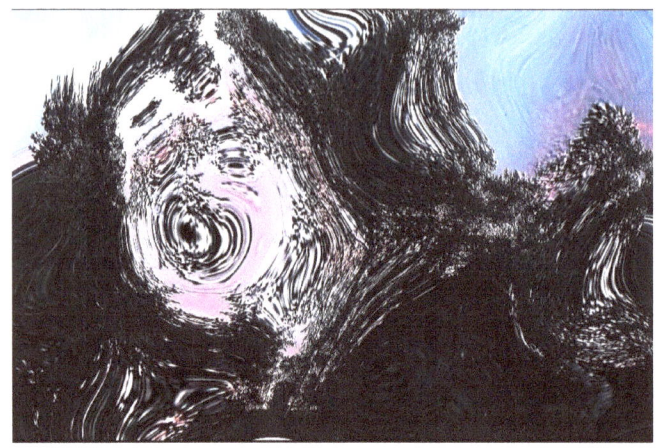

Mania Art by Jennene C. Obremski

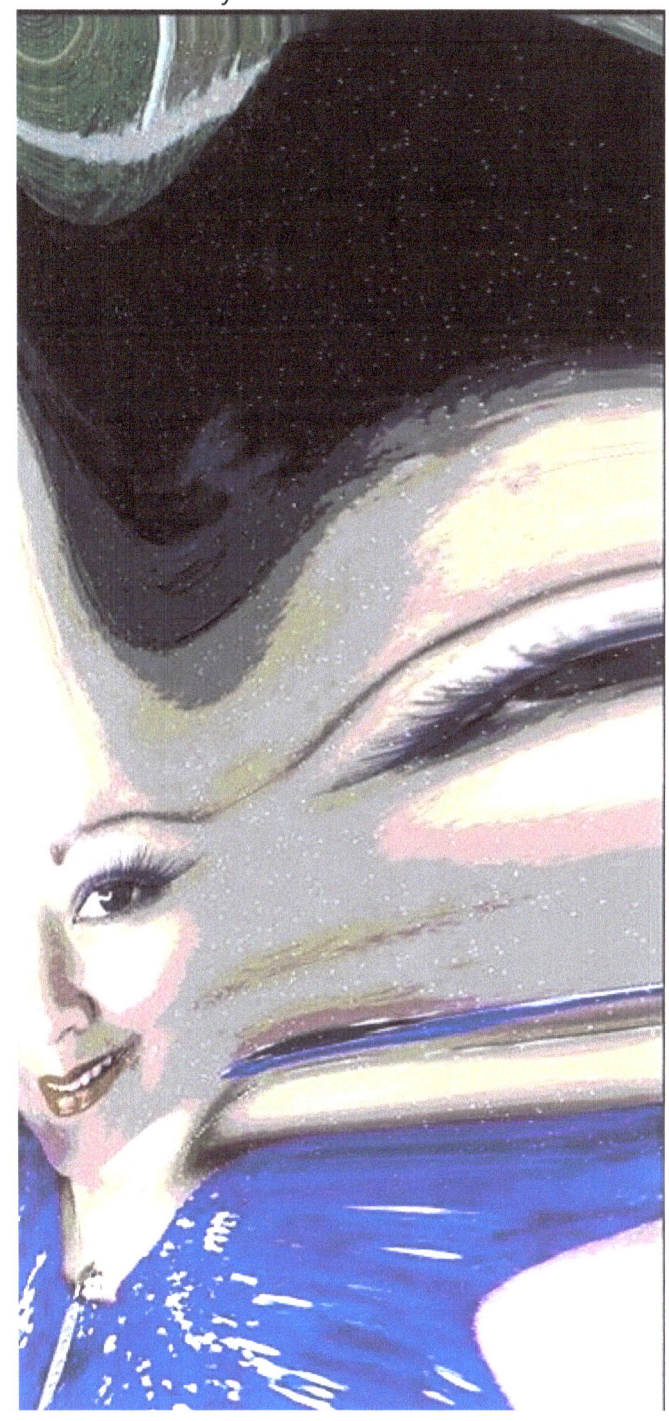

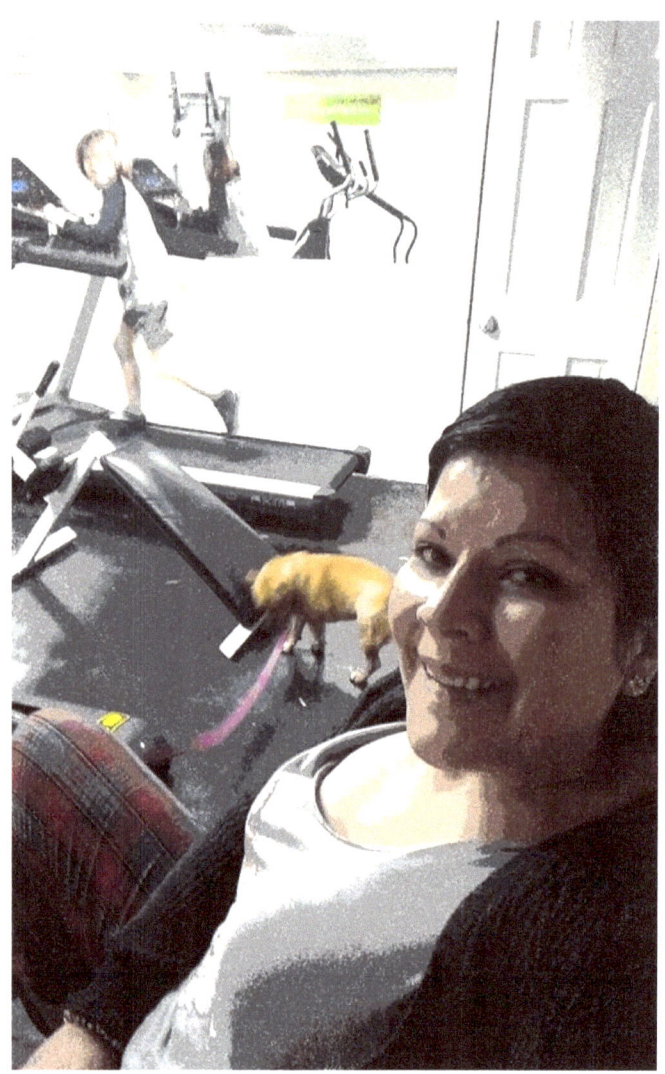

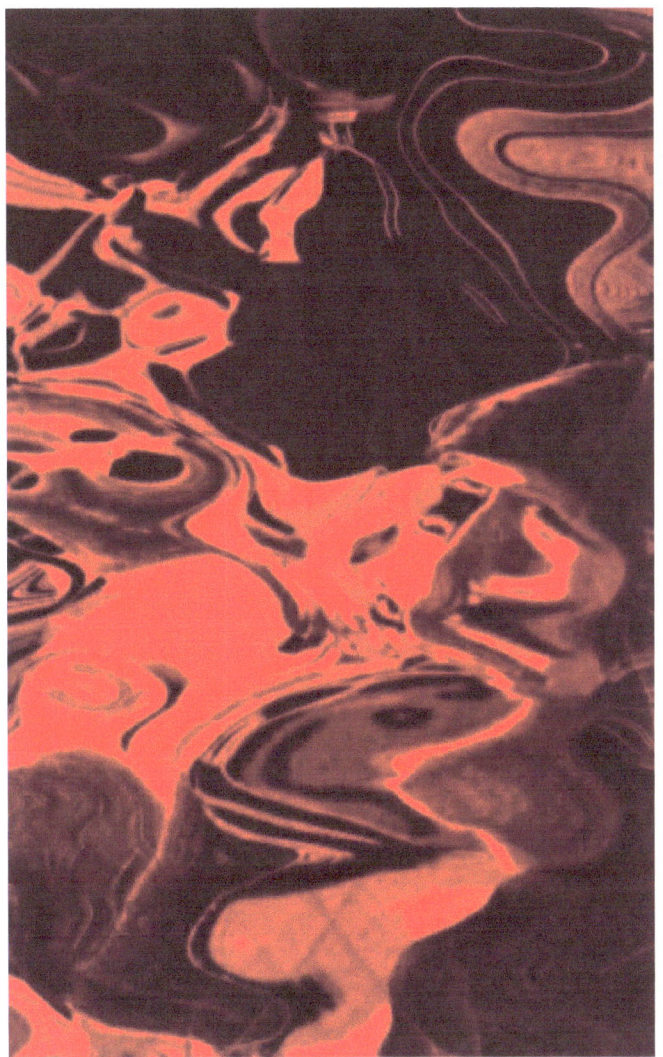

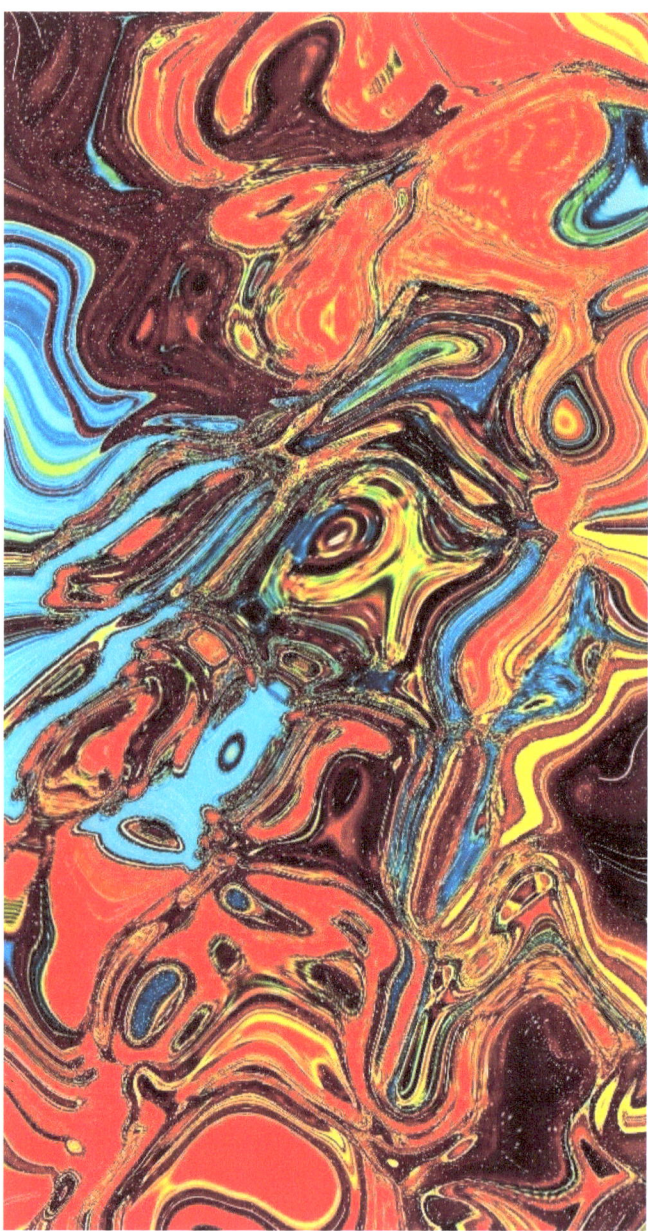

Mania Art by Jennene C. Obremski

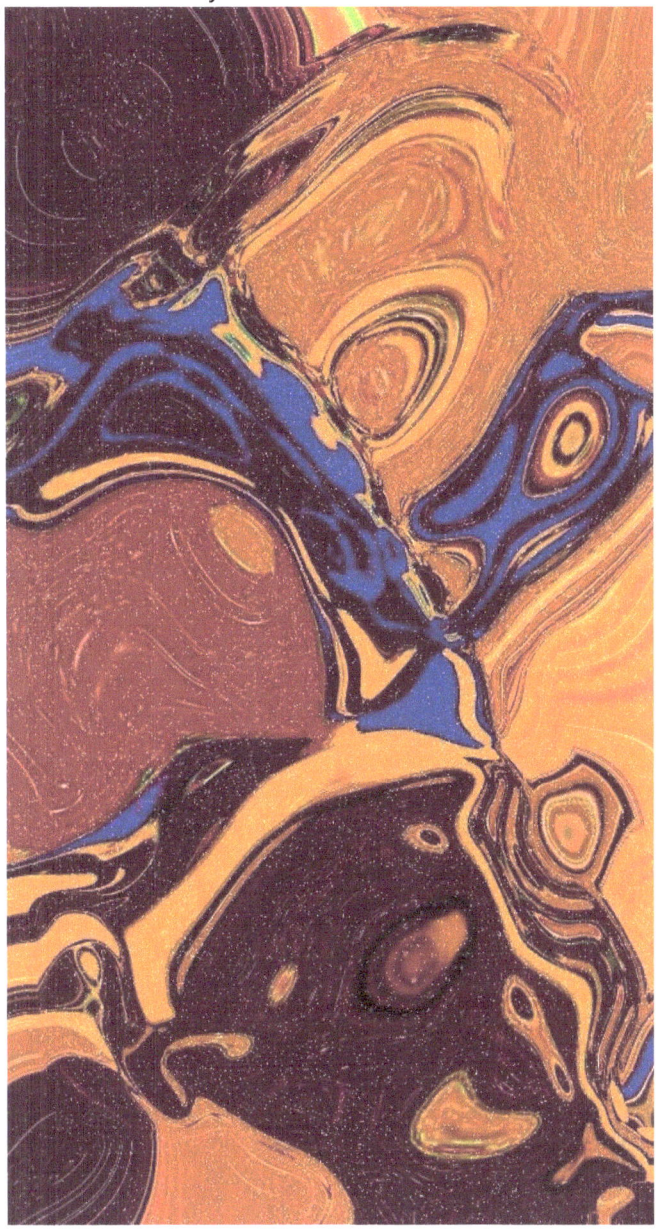

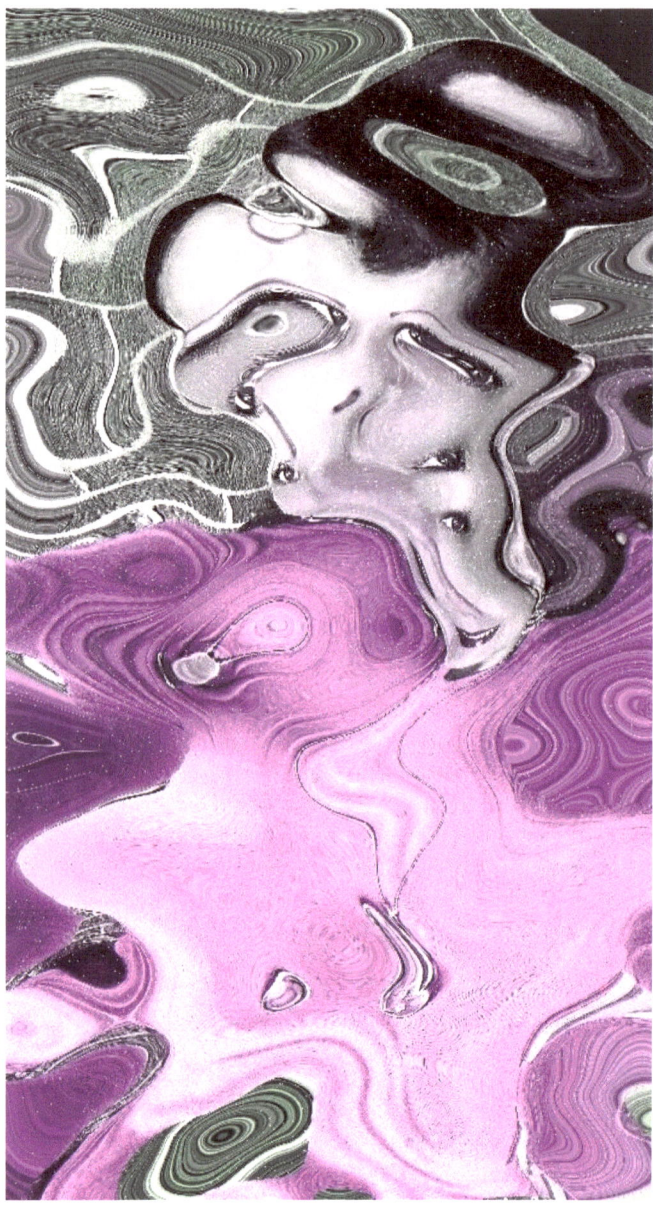

Mania Art by Jennene C. Obremski

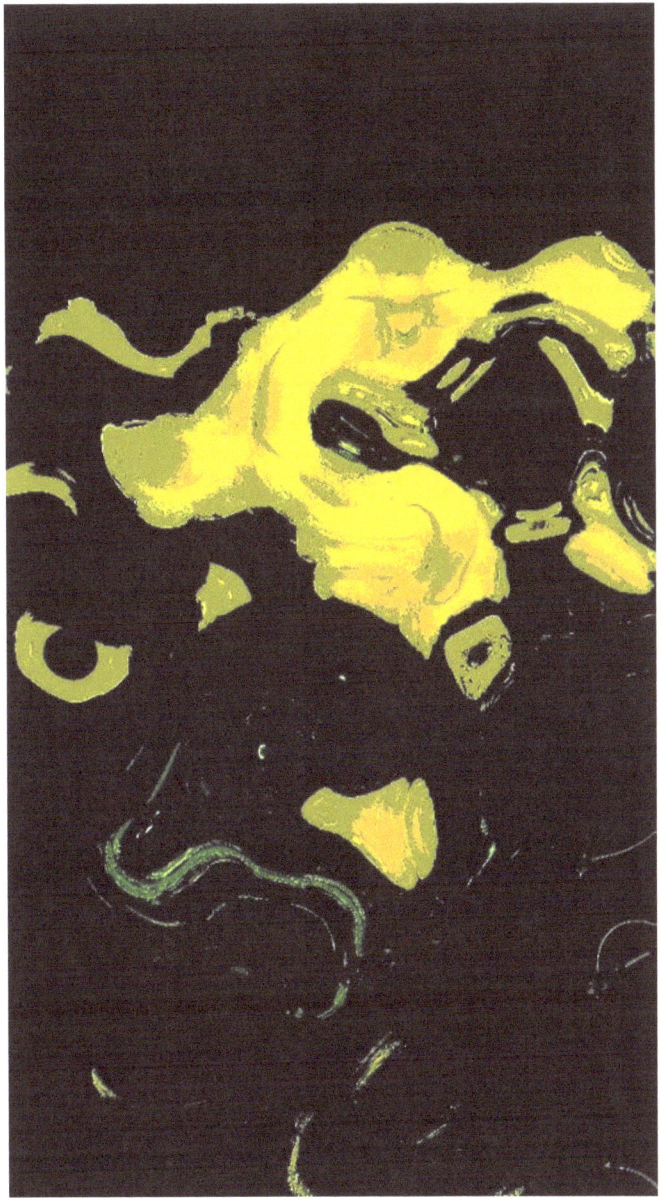

JENNENE OBREMSKI

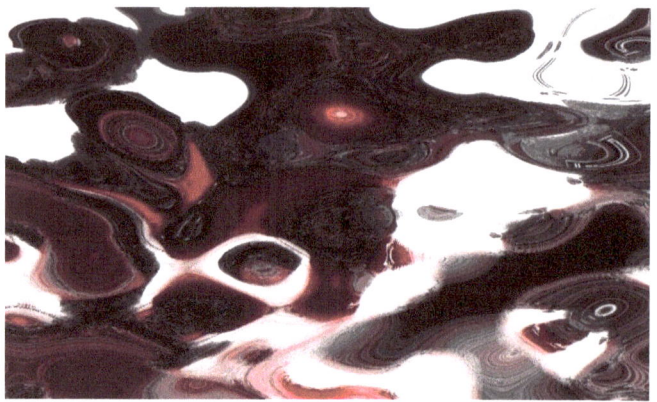

Mania Art by Jennene C. Obremski

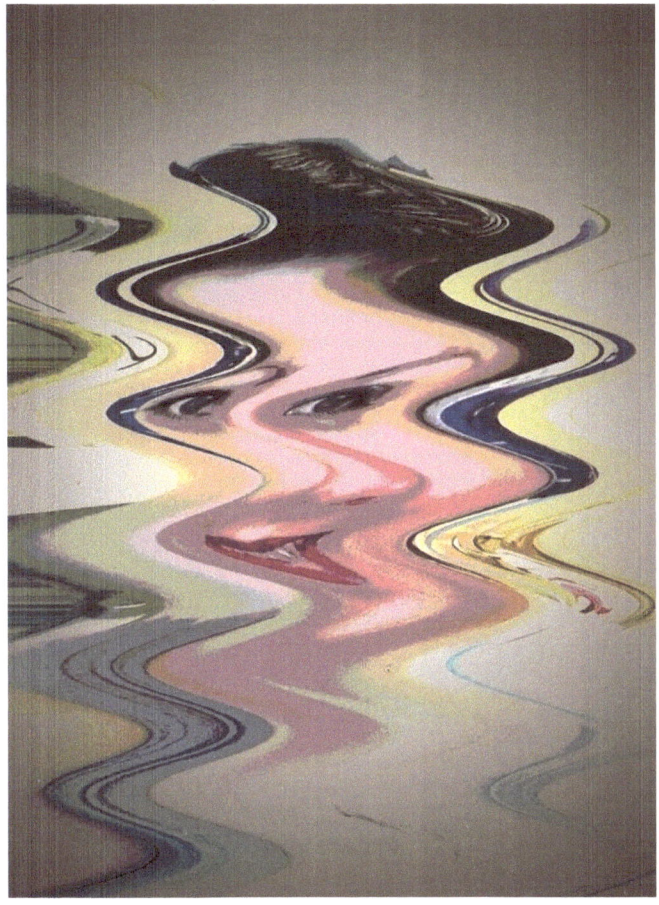

JENNENE OBREMSKI

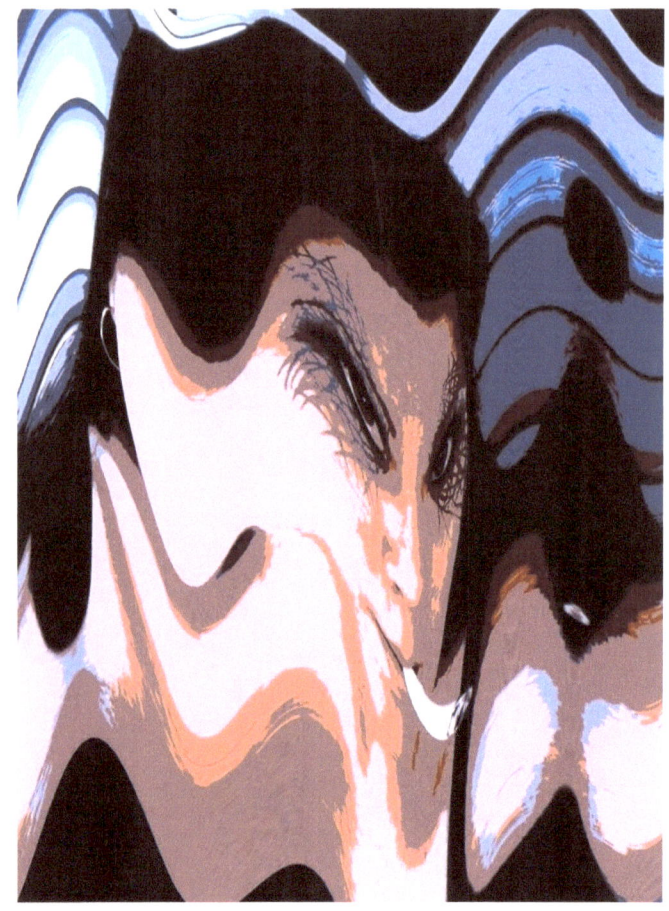

48

Mania Art by Jennene C. Obremski

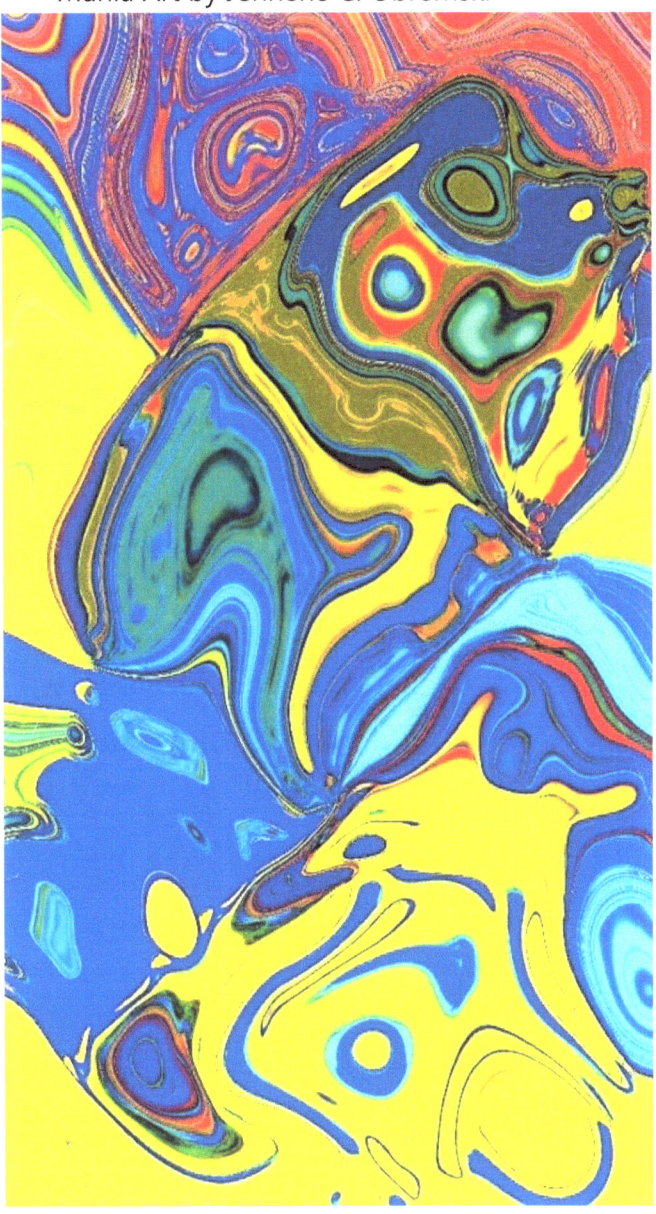

JENNENE OBREMSKI

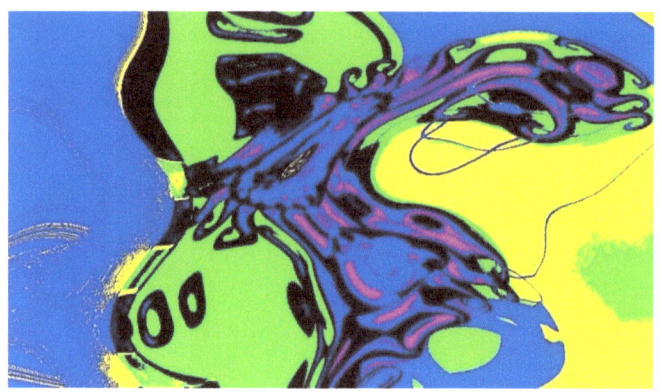

Mania Art by Jennene C. Obremski

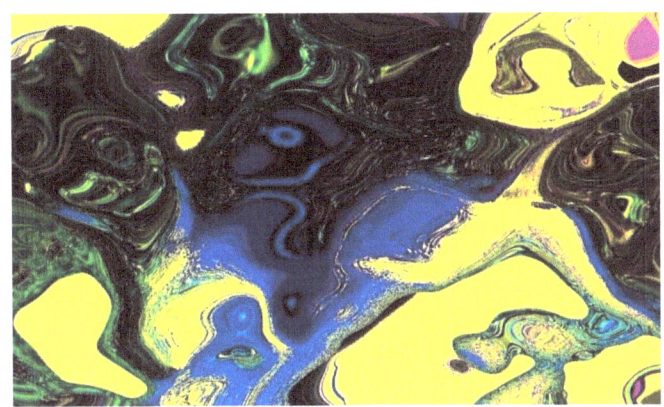

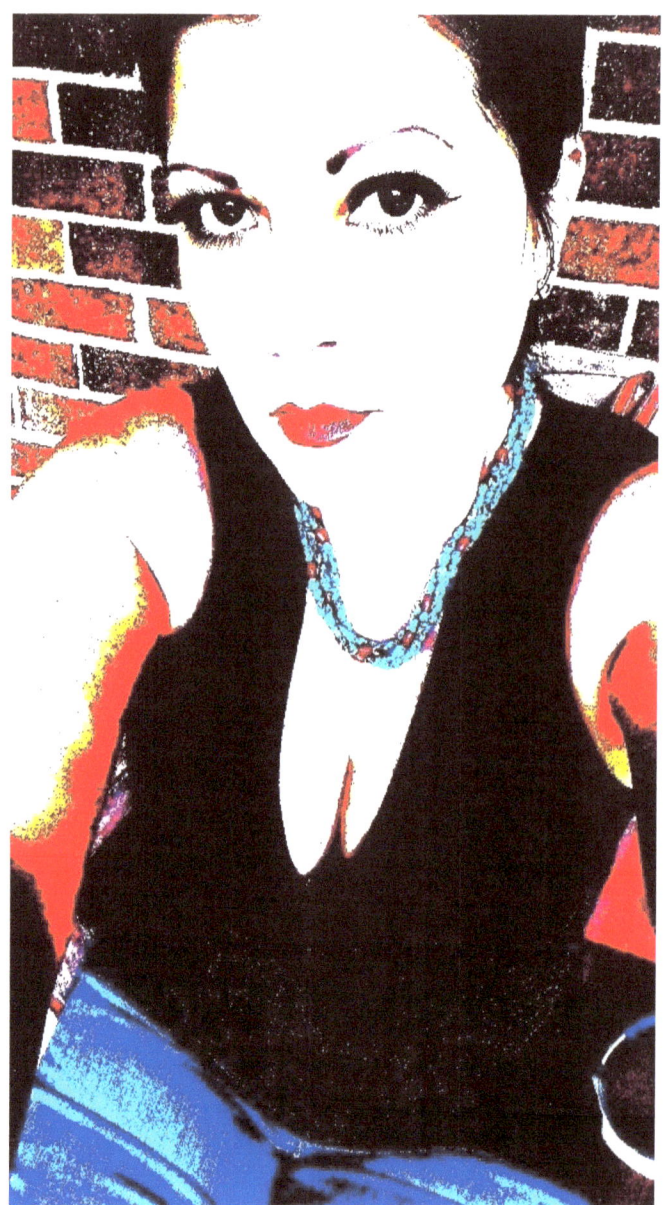

Mania Art by Jennene C. Obremski

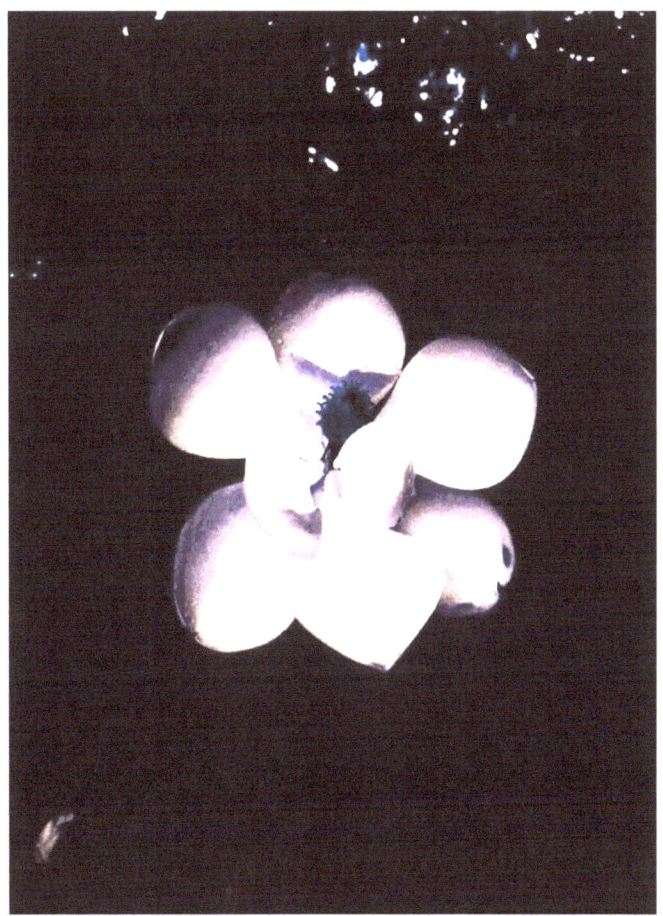

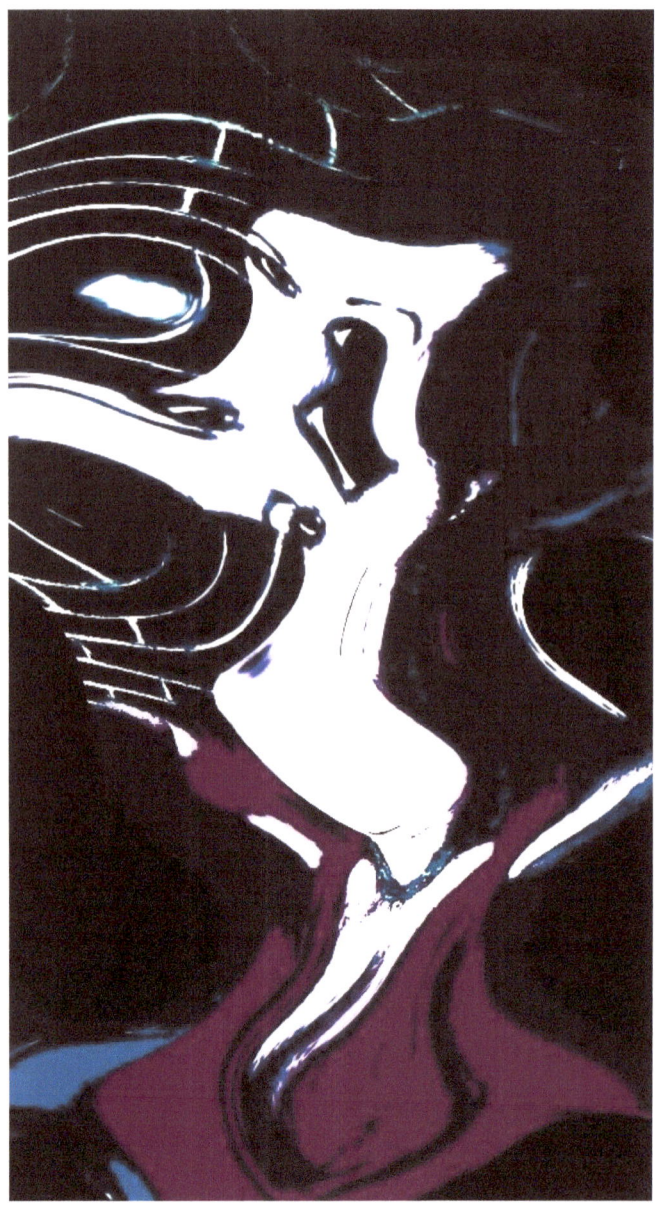

Mania Art by Jennene C. Obremski

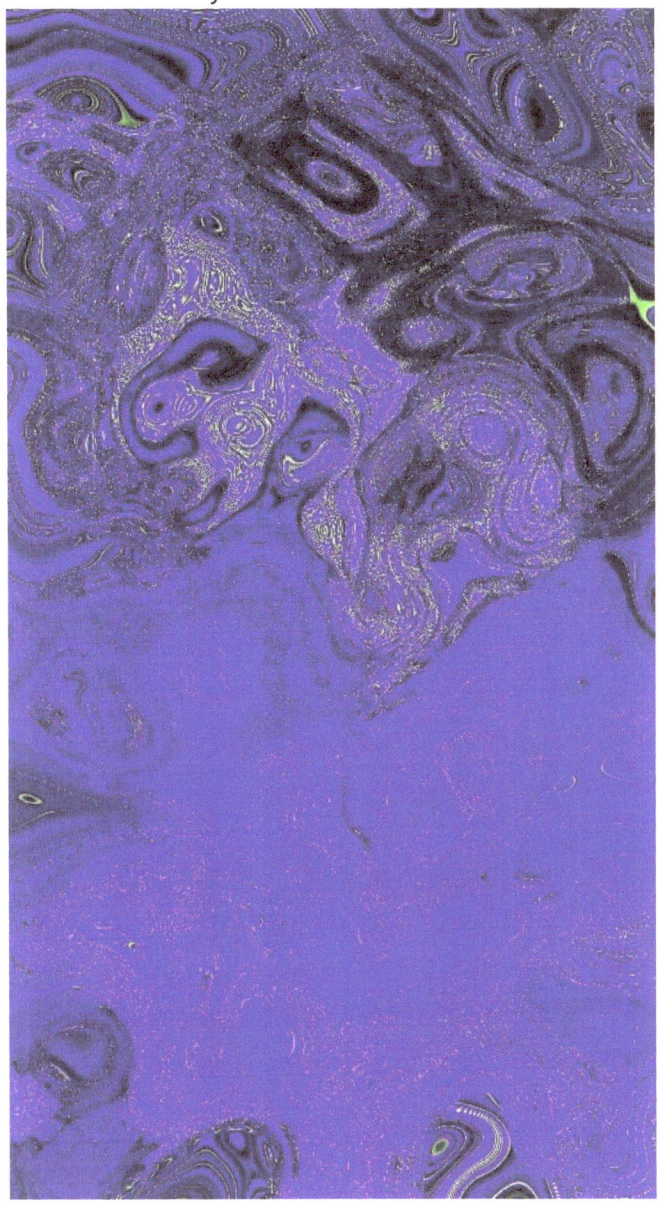

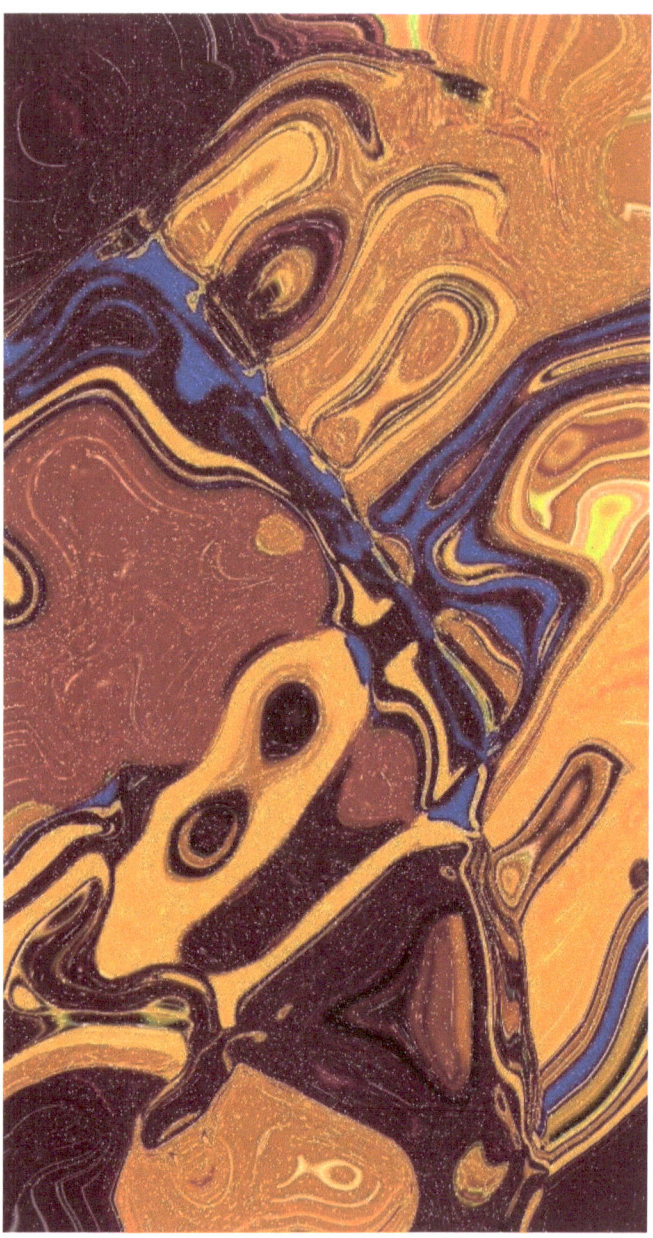

Mania Art by Jennene C. Obremski

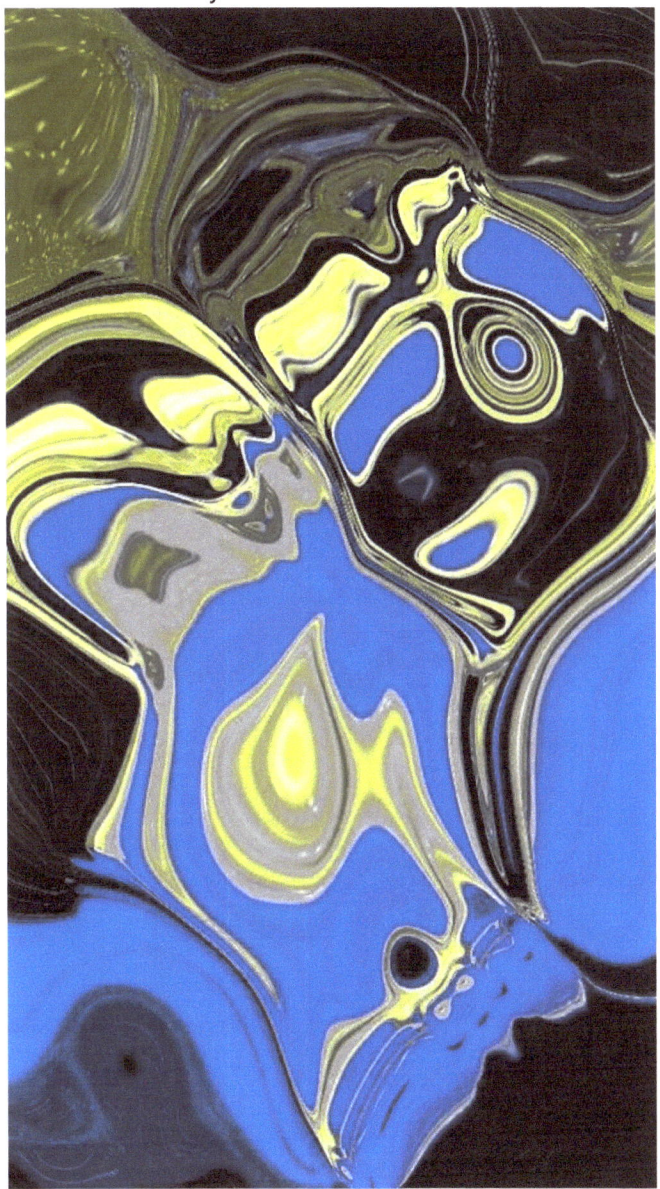

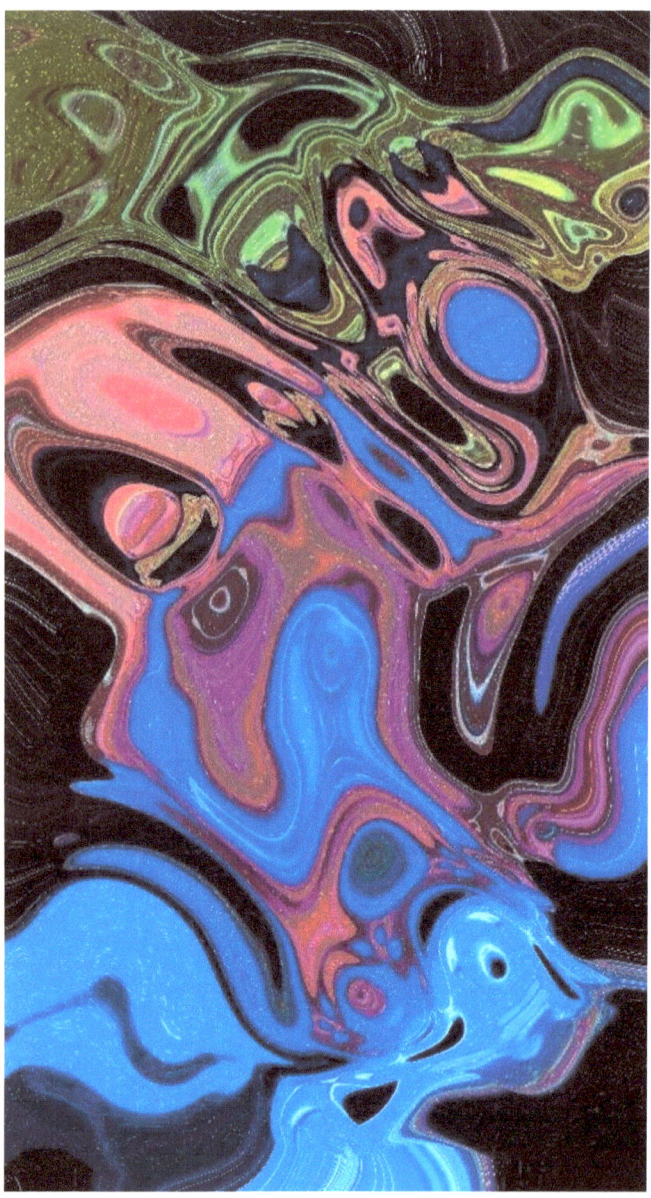

Mania Art by Jennene C. Obremski

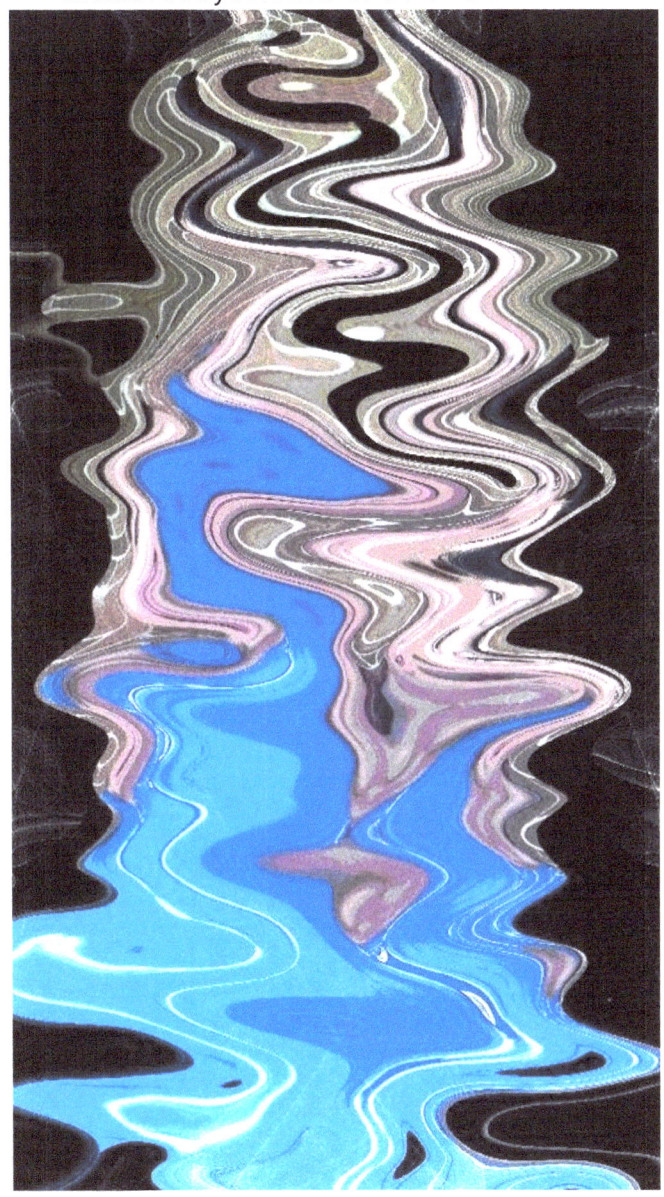

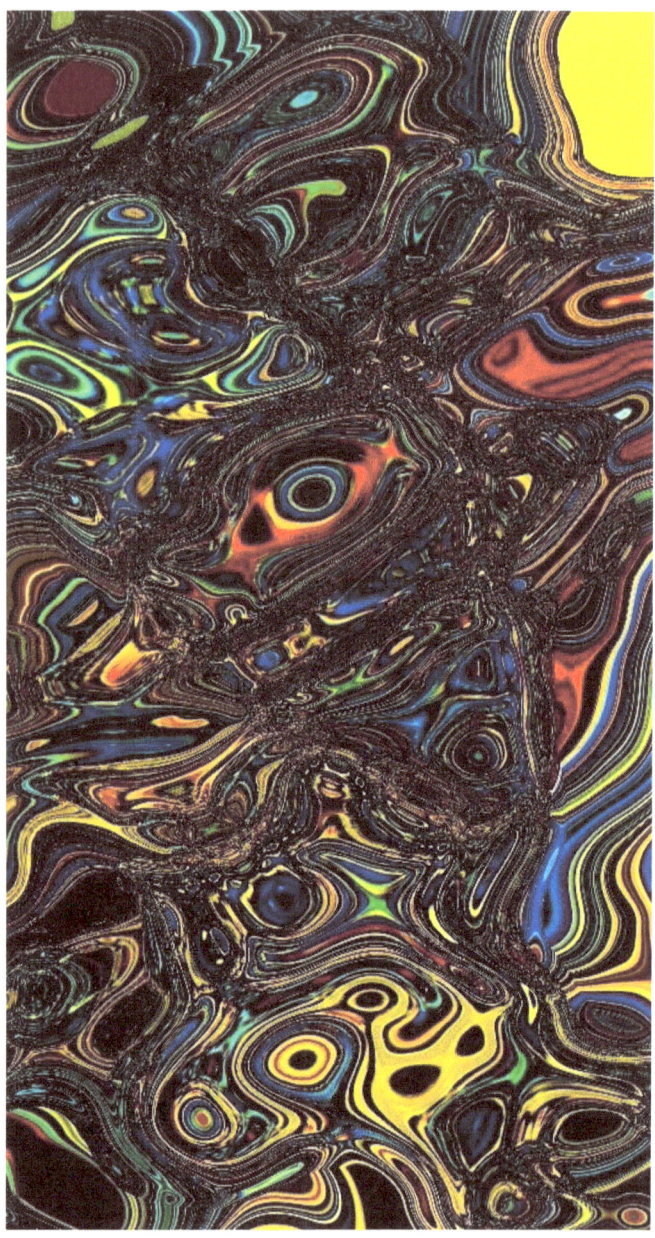

JENNENE OBREMSKI

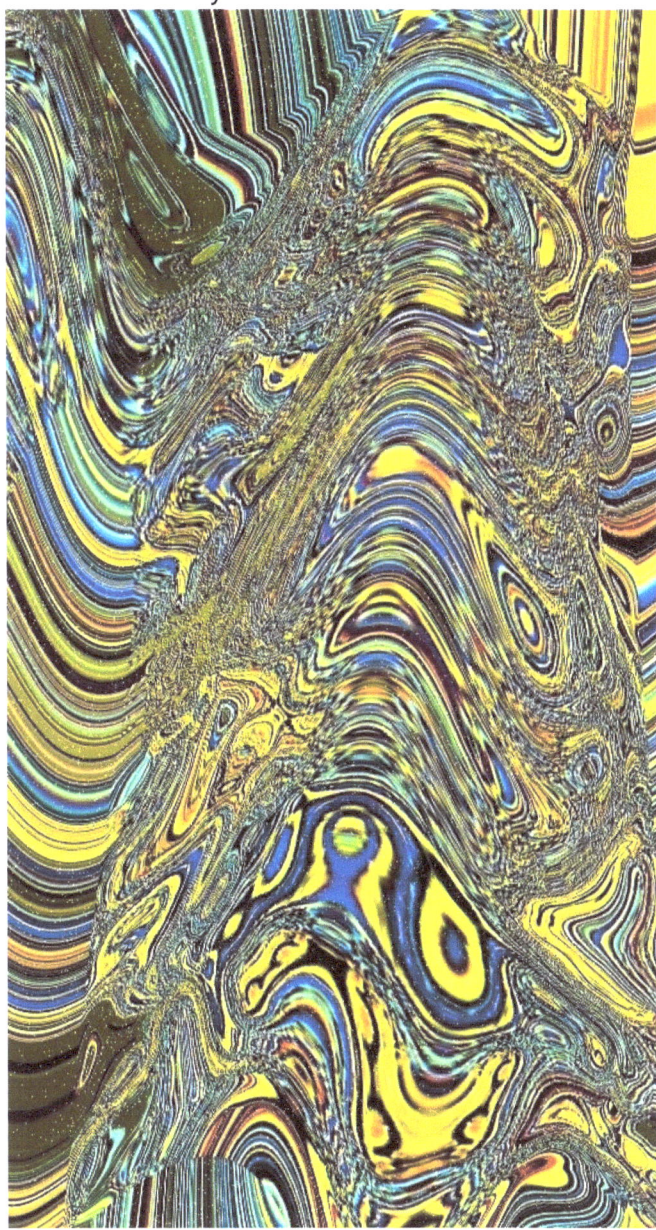

JENNENE OBREMSKI

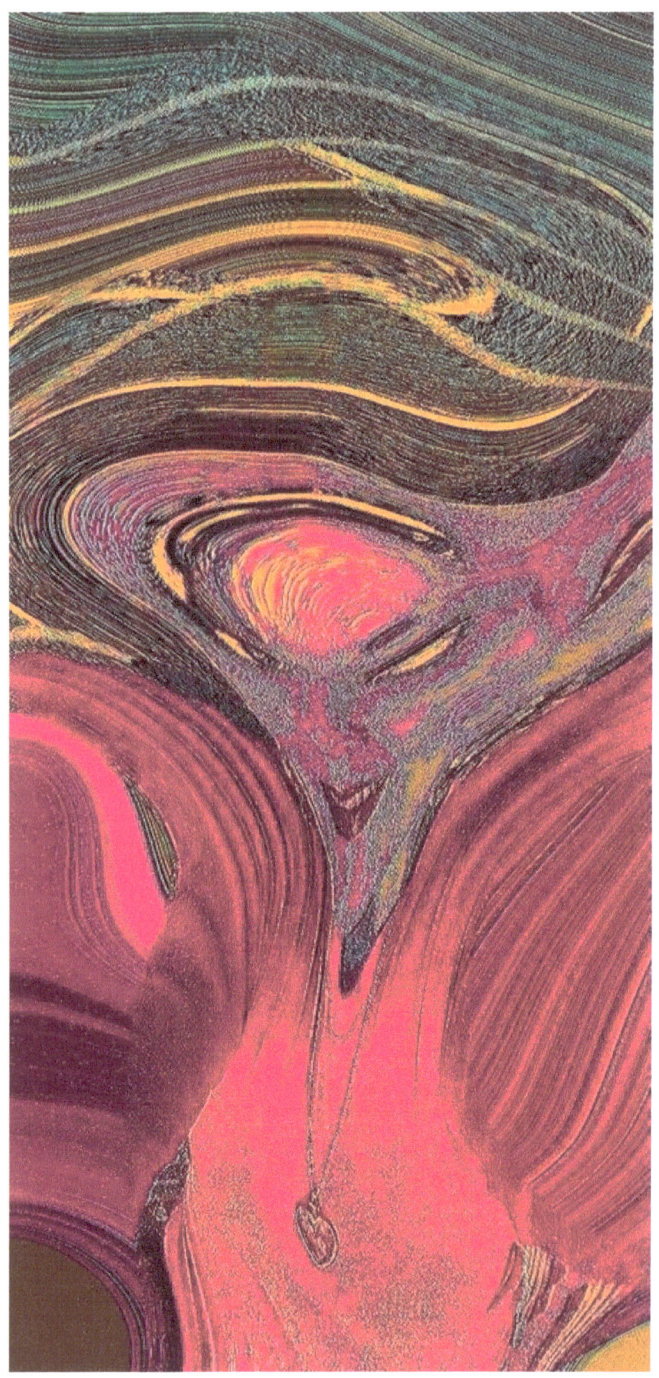

Mania Art by Jennene C. Obremski
Jennene C. Obremski has bipolar 1 and ADHD and has been playing around with photography and her image editor to create these images. She is inspired by Georgia O'Keefe, Vincent Van Gogh Claude Monet, Frida Kahlo and Diego Rivera. She enjoys working on her art while listening to music. A few of her favorites are Nirvana, Sia, Prince, Supertramp, Lily Allen, Amy Whinehouse, Tove Lo, Selena Gomez, Aerosmith, Otis Redding, Corinne Baily Rae, Incubus, Muse, Ella Fitzgerald, Cole Porter, Def Leopard, Motley Crue, Beck, Ludwig Van Bethoven, Pyotr Ilych Tchaikovsky, Blake Shelton, Randy Travis, George Strait, Conway Twitty, Alison Krauss and Dolly Parton. Jennene lives in Maryland with her loving husband of 20 years Ken and their three whip smart kids Andrea, Anthony and Jacob.

JENNENE OBREMSKI

.